SOPHIE DE MULLENHEIM • FABIEN
CHRISTOPHE RAIMBAULT • FRANÇOIS CAMP

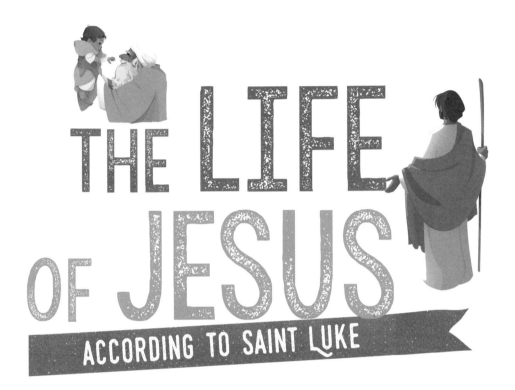

THE LIFE OF JESUS

ACCORDING TO SAINT LUKE

MAGNIFICAT·Ignatius

Contents

Introduction

Jesus really walked this earth. He lived and died and rose from death in real places, in real time. This presentation of his life is based on the Gospel written by Saint Luke, who recounts the words and the deeds of Jesus as told to him by eyewitnesses. In these stories you will discover how Jesus comes to each of us to let us taste God's goodness. What Jesus said to Zacchaeus, who had climbed a tree to see the Lord better, he says to you: *I must stay at your house today* (Luke 19:5). Welcome Jesus! Then you too will experience the adventure of faith in him!

C. Raimbault and F. Campagnac

WHAT IS THE BIBLE?

THE OLD TESTAMENT

A COVENANT STORY

The first part of the Bible, the Old Testament, tells the story of the people of God and foretells the coming of the Messiah, the Savior of the world. It recounts the covenant God established with his chosen people, the Hebrews, now called the Jews. The word "old" here doesn't mean "aged" or "ancient," but "first." As for the Latin word *testamentum*, it means "covenant." The Old Testament is truly the story of the first covenant, the promise between God and his people to love each other for ever.

AN ENTIRE LIBRARY

The Old Testament is a collection of forty-six different books. There are all kinds of texts: poems, epic adventures, prayers, stories, and real historical accounts. Yet, whatever the type of book, they are all considered the Word of God. That doesn't mean God himself wrote them down. Rather, he inspired their authors. The very first stories of the Old Testament were handed down orally over many generations before they were written down by scribes.

THE TORAH, THE HOLY BOOK

The first five books of the Old Testament—Genesis, Exodus, Leviticus, Numbers, and Deuteronomy—are what the Jews call the Torah. These texts form the basis of the Jewish religion. Among them, 613 commandments regulate the life of the Jews. The Torah was written in Hebrew on parchment scrolls that were kept in a precious chest in the Temple. Like all Jews, Jesus studied the Torah and prayed using its texts.

THE PROMISED SAVIOR

In the Old Testament, there are many stories of prophets who spoke to the Jewish people in the name of God. The more time went by, the more they spoke of the Messiah to come, of the Savior God would send to free everyone from sin and death. At the time of Jesus, the Jews were fervently awaiting the Savior. Yet many did not accept Jesus. To this day, Jews still hope for the coming of the Messiah.

A NEW COVENANT

The second part of the Bible, the New Testament, opens with the preaching of John the Baptist and the birth of Jesus. God's promise of a Messiah was fulfilled: he sent his Son to earth to save mankind from sin and death, and to offer a new covenant. This time God invited men and women of all lands to be his people. The Good News of salvation was to spread throughout the world: this was the birth of the Church.

GOOD NEWS FOR ALL PEOPLE

The Bible presents the Good News in four different and complementary texts: these are the four Gospels. "Gospel" is an Old English word meaning "good news." Matthew was one of Jesus' twelve Apostles. He had been a tax collector. His Gospel reveals Jesus as the perfect fulfillment of the promises of the Old Testament. Mark did not know Jesus, but he was a companion of Paul and Barnabas. His Gospel emphasizes Jesus as the Son of God. Luke was a doctor who made a long study of the lives of Jesus and those close to him. His Gospel often speaks of God's mercy. John the Apostle wrote the fourth Gospel. It focuses on Jesus as the Word of God made man, the Son of the Father, who is the source of life, love, and truth.

THE EARLY DAYS OF THE CHURCH

After Jesus' Ascension into heaven, the Apostles were left on their own. These were the first days of the Church, as recounted in the Acts of the Apostles, also written by Luke. Acts is followed by letters written by Saints Paul, Peter, James, and John. All of these letters were sent to support the first Christian communities, to teach them the words of Jesus, and to encourage them in their faith.

THE APOCALYPSE

The very last book of the New Testament, Revelation (or the Apocalypse), is a little scary. It tells of the end of the world, with distress, dragons, and the devil. And yet, it is full of joy as its author, Saint John, reaffirms the victory over evil that Jesus accomplished through his Death and Resurrection. The Book of Revelation was written when Christians were being persecuted. It offers hope to Christians in every age, whenever their faith is put to the test.

The Birth
and Childhood of Jesus

When Mary heard the angel say that she was to give birth to the Savior, she accepted God's will. She went to visit her cousin Elizabeth, who was also expecting a baby, John the Baptist. Jesus was born in Bethlehem in a humble stable in the middle of nowhere. But angels proclaimed to nearby shepherds: this is the One, the awaited Messiah, the Savior of mankind!

The Birth of John Foretold

Luke 1:5-25

TEMPLE SERVICE

The priests in the Jerusalem Temple were descendants of Aaron, the brother of Moses and the high priest of the people. Their office was handed down from father to son. The priests were dedicated to the worship of God. They collected offerings from the faithful and prayed on their behalf by making sacrifices and burning incense. Zechariah was among them. His wife, Elizabeth, was also a descendant of Aaron.

Among the Temple priests was an old man named Zechariah. His wife was called Elizabeth. They were righteous people, faithful to the covenant God had made with their ancestors. Only one thing saddened them: they had no children. One day, while Zechariah was in the Temple offering incense, the angel Gabriel, a messenger of God, appeared to him.

The angel said, *Do not be afraid, Zechariah, for your prayer is heard, and your wife Elizabeth will bear you a son, and you shall call his name John* (1:13). The angel explained that many would rejoice at the birth of John. He would be a great prophet, and his mission would be to prepare the people for the coming of the Savior promised by God, the **Messiah**.

Zechariah couldn't believe his ears. "What proof do I have that this is true?" he asked. And the angel answered him, "Since you have doubted my words, you will be unable to speak until the birth of the child. This will be a sign to you that I have come on behalf of God!" Unable to speak, Zechariah left the Temple making wild gestures, and the people gathered outside understood that God must have sent him a message.

Zechariah returned home to Elizabeth. A few months later, Elizabeth whispered to him, "I know it's hard to believe, but I'm going to have a baby!"

WHAT KIND OF MESSIAH?

All the Jews were awaiting the Messiah, which means "the anointed one." For indeed, God had promised to send his Messiah to save mankind. He announced his coming through the prophets (for example, Hosea, Micah, Isaiah, and Jeremiah). The people of Israel expected a great king who would free them from Roman occupation, but instead the Savior was born to simple people. The long-awaited Messiah did not come amid fanfare; instead he was born in a lowly stable.

The Annunciation

Luke 1:26-38

"Conceive and bear a son"

Mary was going to conceive a child: she would become pregnant. Then she would bear a son: she would give birth.

"House of Jacob"

This means all the Jewish people, all the descendants of the twelve sons of Jacob.

In the town of Nazareth, in Galilee, lived a young woman called Mary. She was soon to be married to Joseph, a distant descendant of the great King David. One day, God sent the angel Gabriel to Mary's home.

"Hail, Mary, full of grace," he said to her, "the Lord is with you!"

Mary was startled by this strange greeting and wondered what it could mean.

But the angel said to her, *Do not be afraid, Mary, for you have found favor with God. And behold, you will **conceive** in your womb and **bear a son**, and you shall call his name Jesus. He will be great and will be called the Son of the Most High; and the Lord God will give to him the throne of his father David, and he will reign over the **house of Jacob** for ever; and of his kingdom there will be no end* (1:30-33).

WHO ARE YOU, MARY?

The Bible tells us little about Mary, and yet she played a central role in our salvation. Her "Yes" to God made the life of Jesus possible. Mary is the foremost model of faith in God. Through her words and deeds, she teaches us to listen to Jesus and to do what he says.

Mary replied, "How will this be, since I'm not married yet?"

And the angel said to her, "The Holy Spirit will come upon you, for the child you are to bear is the Son of God. And behold, God has given your elderly cousin Elizabeth a wonderful gift as well: she too is expecting a son! For with God, nothing is impossible." And Mary said, "Yes! I am the servant of the Lord; I trust in him and wish to serve him all the days of my life. May all this come to pass for me just as you say."

MARY, HELP US TO SAY YES!

Like all Jews of her time, Mary was awaiting the coming of the Messiah. She was preparing for it through prayer and trust. The angel's announcement no doubt surprised her: she wasn't expecting to be chosen to bear the Messiah! But her heart was pure and had long been ready, for she was without sin; and she was able to say yes to God's plan for her.

At Mass, before you receive Communion, you can ask Mary to help you to prepare your heart for Jesus so that you too are ready to receive him, as she was.

15

HAIL, MARY

The Hail Mary begins with the words of the Annunciation: "Hail, Mary, full of grace, the Lord is with thee." It continues with Elizabeth's words at the Visitation: "Blessed art thou among women, and blessed is the fruit of thy womb." The final part was added in 1568, but long before then Christians had been asking Mary for her prayers.

THANK YOU, LORD

Mary was astonished to have been chosen by God to bear his Son. In the presence of Elizabeth, she sings the beautiful words of the *Magnificat*. She expresses her joy and gives thanks to God for having blessed one so humble as herself.

When you receive Communion, God humbles himself to come to you! At each Communion, borrow Mary's words to express your thanks and joy for the gift of Jesus.

Mary set out at once to visit Elizabeth. Upon seeing Mary, Elizabeth was deeply moved and exclaimed, "Blessed are you among women, and blessed is the fruit of your womb! For the moment I heard your greeting, the child in my womb leaped for joy. Blessed are you who believed and trusted in the Lord."

Mary responded with her *Magnificat*, her great canticle of praise to God:

My soul magnifies the Lord,
and my spirit rejoices in God my Savior,
for he has looked with favor on his lowly servant.
From this day all generations will call me blessed because the Almighty has done great things for me and holy is his name.
He has mercy on those who fear him
in every generation.
He has shown the strength of his arm
and scattered the proud-hearted.
He has brought down the mighty from their thrones and lifted up the lowly.
He has filled the hungry with good things
and sent the rich away empty.
He has come to the help of his servant Israel,
remembering his promise of mercy,
which he made to our fathers,
to Abraham and his children for ever.

The Birth of John

Luke 1:57-80

Elizabeth gave birth to a beautiful baby boy. According to Jewish tradition, he was to be **circumcised** eight days after birth and given his name. Family and friends wanted to call him Zechariah, after his father, but Elizabeth refused: *Not so; he shall be called John* (1:60). Then they asked Zechariah his opinion. Since he was still unable to speak, he took a writing tablet and wrote, *His name is John* (1:63). At that very moment, he regained the power of speech! He gave thanks to God, saying, "Lord, you are faithful to your covenant and have come to save us, just as you promised!" Those present were amazed and said: "This indeed is an extraordinary child! God will surely accomplish wonderful things through him!"

"Circumcision"
Circumcision is a little operation to remove a baby boy's foreskin. It is a ceremony that marks a child's entrance into the covenant between God and the people of Israel.

HIS NAME IS JOHN

Jewish children are given their name eight days after birth. It is normally the father who chooses the name. Everyone imagined that Elizabeth's baby would be called Zechariah, after his father. But when Zechariah had doubted the angel's promise, he became mute. So it was Elizabeth who told the priest, "He will be named John," which Zechariah confirmed in writing. The name John means "God is gracious."

The Birth of Jesus

Luke 2:1-21

THE CRÈCHE

Crèche is the French word for "manger," a trough that holds food for farm animals. According to the Gospel of Luke, baby Jesus was laid in a manger because there was no room for his family at the inn. Today, the word "crèche" is used for a Nativity scene that represents the birth of Jesus with little figurines. In 1223, Saint Francis of Assisi, Italy, created the first crèche with live people and animals. Even though the Gospels don't mention a donkey and an ox at the first Christmas, we often place them in the crèche because of a verse in the Book of Isaiah (Isaiah 1:3).

When the Roman emperor decided to count all the inhabitants of his empire, everyone had to travel to his native city to enroll his name in a great register. Joseph himself left Nazareth for Bethlehem, the city of King David—taking with him his wife, Mary, who was soon to have a baby. What a hard journey for an expectant mother! When they arrived in Bethlehem, there was no more room at the inn. They found shelter in a stable, and there Jesus was born. Mary wrapped her newborn in swaddling clothes to keep him warm, and laid him in the animals' manger.

That night there were shepherds in the nearby fields keeping watch over their flocks. The angel of the Lord appeared before them, and the glory of the Lord shone around them. They were seized with great fear.

A SHEPHERD'S LIFE

Shepherds were a common sight in Jesus' time. They watched over flocks of sheep and goats. They led them to pasture and water, nursed them, and guarded them at night to keep wild animals away. They helped with the birthing of lambs, and they were careful that no animal went astray. Shepherds worked very hard. They did a tough job and were respected. Did you know that some very great biblical figures were shepherds? These included Abraham, Moses, and even King David.

The angel said to them, "Be not afraid; for behold, I bring you good news of a great joy which will come to all the people; for to you is born this day in the city of David a Savior, who is Christ the Lord. And this will be a sign for you: you will find a baby wrapped in swaddling cloths and lying in a manger." And suddenly there was with the angel a multitude of the heavenly host praising God and saying, "Glory to God in the highest, and on earth peace among men with whom he is pleased!" (2:10-14).

At that, the shepherds said to one another, "Quick, let's go to Bethlehem and see what's happening!" They found Mary, Joseph, and their newborn baby. With great joy, they praised God. On the eighth day, the baby was circumcised and was given the name Jesus, which means "God saves."

GLORY TO GOD!

At Mass, right after we ask and receive God's forgiveness, we repeat the angels' words at the birth of Jesus: "Glory to God in the highest, and on earth peace to people of good will." This is our way of giving thanks to the Lord for forgiving our sins, for loving us despite our faults, and for offering himself to us in the Eucharist.

STRANGE GIFTS!

In the Gospel of Matthew, Magi, wise men from the East, visited the baby Jesus. They brought strange gifts for such a humble child: gold, frankincense, and myrrh. Gold is a gift for kings; frankincense is an aromatic plant resin burned in religious worship; myrrh, another fragrant resin, was used to anoint the dead. To Christians, these gifts explain who Jesus really is: King of kings, Lord of lords, and God made man to share in human suffering and death.

The Presentation

Luke 2:22-38

THE PRESENTATION IN THE TEMPLE

Jewish Law requires that every firstborn male be consecrated to the Lord (Exodus 13:2). In the time of Jesus, when a firstborn son was forty days old, his father presented him to God in the Temple and "ransomed" him, or bought him back, by offering the priest a sum of money. The mother, for her part, offered a sacrifice for her purification after childbirth. The richest women would bring a lamb and a pigeon in offering. Others, like Mary, were only able to offer a pair of pigeons or turtledoves.

Obeying the Law of Moses, Mary and Joseph brought baby Jesus to the Jerusalem Temple to dedicate him to the Lord. When they entered the Temple, an old man approached them. His name was Simeon, and he had been waiting a long time for the Messiah to appear. As soon as he saw Jesus, Simeon knew in his heart that he was the Savior sent by God. Deeply moved, he took the baby in his arms, blessed God, and said, "Lord, now let your servant go in peace, for my eyes have seen your salvation, a light to reveal you to the nations."

Mary and Joseph were astonished.

Jesus Lost and Found Again

Luke 2:41-52

Every year for the feast of Passover, Mary and Joseph would travel on pilgrimage to the Temple in Jerusalem with others from their village. When Jesus was twelve years old, he went with them. What an adventure! And what joy to see this magnificent Temple, the dwelling place of God!

As they were returning home, Mary and Joseph couldn't see Jesus. But they said to themselves, "He must be walking ahead with his friends." However, the next day there was still no Jesus in sight! Frantic with worry, Mary and Joseph hurried back to Jerusalem and scoured the whole city looking for him.

At last they found him in the Temple courtyard, where the **doctors of the Law** gathered to debate. Jesus was listening to them and asking them questions. The people were amazed at his intelligence. Overcome with relief, Mary said to her son, "What a fright you gave us! Why did you do this to us?"

And he replied, *How is it that you sought me? Did you not know that I must be in my Father's house?* (2:49).

Mary and Joseph were puzzled by what he said, but Jesus went back with them to Nazareth. There he obeyed his parents and grew up in strength and wisdom.

THE DOCTORS OF THE LAW

Men responsible for writing down the Law on parchment scrolls were called doctors of the Law, or scribes. They would read these texts, study them, and explain them to the faithful in long sermons. People came to them for advice about difficult questions, and their opinions were respected. Like all Jews of his time, Jesus listened attentively to the teachings of the scribes, but he surprised them by his understanding of the Law, which was even greater and more astute than theirs.

THE LAND OF ISRAEL

A LAND OCCUPIED BY THE ROMANS

UNDER ROMAN OCCUPATION

In 63 B.C., General Pompey invaded Judea in the name of the Roman Empire. He captured Jerusalem and imposed Roman law on the country. The Romans sent their own governors and appointed a king in Judea, Herod the Great. Herod was detested by all, for he was cruel and was cooperating with the enemy. On his death, shortly after the birth of Jesus, his son Herod Antipas began to rule, and Galilee regained a certain amount of independence. Judea and Jerusalem, however, remained under tight Roman control. Emperor Tiberias sent a new Roman governor in the year A.D. 26: Pontius Pilate. He didn't realize the importance of religion in the country. Not understanding the Jewish way of life, he made many blunders that stirred up the people against him.

A DETESTED OCCUPIER

Life was very hard for the Jews under Roman occupation. They were crushed by taxes on land, people, harvests, and goods. They regularly suffered humiliation for their beliefs by an occupier who didn't respect their traditions or their holy sites. Revolts to push out the occupiers increasingly shook the land. The Zealots, for example, formed armed bands to attack the Romans. But above all, the Jews awaited the Messiah foretold by the prophets. The time of his coming was near, they were sure of it, and they hoped for a king who would save them from their oppressors.

A RELIGIOUS TRIBUNAL

The Roman occupiers controlled everything in the land except religion. A religious tribunal handled matters of the faith and made judgments according to Jewish Law. This tribunal, called the Sanhedrin, was made up of seventy elders or scribes and was presided over by the high priest of the Temple. The Sanhedrin passed laws, judged those who broke the Law, certified marriages, and administered a religious tax. When Jesus was accused of blasphemy, he was brought before this tribunal for judgment.

① This is the village where Jesus was born.

② Jesus grew up in Nazareth and worked here as a carpenter.

③ Jesus was baptized in the waters of the Jordan River by his cousin John the Baptist.

④ The fishermen Peter and Andrew met the Messiah on the banks of the Sea of Galilee.

⑤ Jesus preached in the synagogue in Capernaum. In this city he also cured the sick servant of a Roman centurion.

⑥ Peter, James, and John witnessed the Transfiguration on Mount Tabor.

⑦ Jerusalem is the capital and center of religious life in the land of Israel. Jesus was condemned to death and crucified there.

⑧ On the road from Jerusalem to Emmaus, the risen Jesus met two of his disciples.

⑨ The Apostles were present at Jesus' Ascension near the village of Bethany.

GALILEE

⑤ Capernaum

Sea of Galilee

④

② Nazareth

⑥ Mount Tabor

DECAPOLIS

Caesarea

SAMARIA

Jordan River

③

PEREA

Mediterranean Sea

⑧ Emmaus

⑦ Jerusalem

⑨ Bethany

① Bethlehem

JUDEA

Dead Sea

N
W E
S

Jesus
Begins His Mission

When he became an adult, Jesus began his mission. After John baptized him, he confronted temptation and emerged victorious from the struggle. He spoke of God his Father to the people he met. He proclaimed the Good News, the Gospel, by showing the love and mercy of God to those around him, especially by healing the sick. To help him in his mission, Jesus chose twelve Apostles, special friends who followed him and listened to his teaching for three years.

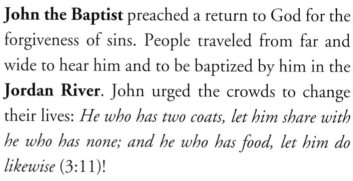

JOHN THE BAPTIST

John proclaimed the coming of the Messiah: *Prepare the way of the Lord!* (3:4). Clothed in animal skins, he lived on locusts and wild honey. Crowds flocked to him to be baptized. Many disciples followed him, including Andrew, the brother of Peter, and both of them became Apostles of Jesus. But John's preaching irritated the powerful, and King Herod, whose bad behavior John criticized, had him beheaded.

John the Baptist preached a return to God for the forgiveness of sins. People traveled from far and wide to hear him and to be baptized by him in the **Jordan River**. John urged the crowds to change their lives: *He who has two coats, let him share with he who has none; and he who has food, let him do likewise* (3:11)!

As people listened to him, they wondered, "Is John perhaps the Messiah we've been waiting for? The Christ?"

But John said to them, *I baptize you with water; but he who is mightier than I is coming, the thong of whose sandals I am not worthy to untie; he will baptize you with the Holy Spirit and with fire* (3:16).

Soon afterward Jesus arrived to be baptized. And as he was praying, the Holy Spirit descended upon him in the form of a dove. Then a voice thundered from heaven, saying, *You are my beloved Son; with you I am well pleased* (3:22).

THE JORDAN RIVER

The Jordan has its source in the mountains of Lebanon and flows into the Dead Sea. The crossing of this river marked the entry of the Hebrews into the Promised Land. To be immersed in the waters of the Jordan, and today in baptismal water, is to be born into new life.

The Temptation in the Desert

Luke 4:1-13

Jesus, filled with the Holy Spirit, withdrew into the desert, where he prayed and fasted for forty days. When he was very hungry, the devil tried to tempt him: *If you are the Son of God, command this stone to become bread* (4:3).

And Jesus answered, *It is written, "Man shall not live by bread alone"* (4:4).

The devil showed Jesus all the kingdoms of the world, and said to him, "I will give you all of this if you worship me." And Jesus answered, *It is written, "You shall worship the Lord your God, and him only shall you serve"* (4:8).

Then the devil took Jesus to the top of the Temple. "Throw yourself down from here," he said, "for it is written that the angels will protect you." And Jesus answered, *It is said, "You shall not tempt the Lord your God"* (4:12).

With that, the devil fled!

JESUS IN THE DESERT

Galilee, the land of Jesus, is a lush, green country where water flows in abundance. Judea, on the other hand, is a barren land with arid mountains. It was there that Jesus chose to withdraw before beginning his public ministry. He went to the desert to pray and fast. He remained there for forty days, just as the Hebrew people had spent forty years in the desert before entering the Promised Land. Lent also lasts forty days so that we can pray and fast with Jesus to prepare our hearts for the great joy of Easter.

Jesus in Nazareth

Luke 4:16-30

THE SABBATH

The sabbath is a day consecrated to God. It falls on the seventh day of the week, Saturday. For Jews, this is a day of rest and prayer in memory of God's rest after the six days of creation. The Law of Moses states that no work may be done on that day.

On the sabbath day, Jews gather in the synagogue to worship God. The service begins with a prayer; then there is a reading from the Law of Moses, followed by a text from the prophets. Psalms are also sung. A rabbi explains the readings. That is what Jesus did in the Nazareth synagogue.

Jesus returned to Nazareth, the village of his childhood. On the **sabbath** day, he went to the **synagogue** and stepped forward to give a reading from the Scriptures. In the scroll, he read this passage from the prophet Isaiah: *The Spirit of the Lord is upon me, because he has anointed me to preach good news to the poor. He has sent me to proclaim release to the captives and recovering of sight to the blind, to set at liberty those who are oppressed, to proclaim the acceptable year of the Lord* (4:18-19).

Then he put the scroll aside and said, *Today this Scripture has been fulfilled in your hearing* (4:21). Everyone was astonished. "Is he not Joseph's son?" they said. "How can he say that he has been sent by God?" Jesus said, "I suppose now you expect me to work miracles. But no prophet is accepted in his native land." On hearing this, the people became furious. They shoved him out of the city and led him to the top of a hill. They were about to throw him off the cliff, but Jesus eluded them and went on his way.

Jesus in Capernaum

Luke 4:31-44

Jesus went to Capernaum, and on the sabbath he entered the synagogue and taught the people. Many were impressed by his words, which he spoke with authority. Then a man possessed by an **evil spirit** began shouting, *Ah! What have you to do with us, Jesus of Nazareth? Have you come to destroy us? I know who you are, the Holy One of God* (4:34).

Jesus rebuked the demon, saying, *Be silent, and come out of him!* (4:35). And with that, the demon came out of the man. The crowd was amazed. "Who is this Jesus who even commands evil spirits?" they wondered.

A little later, Simon Peter's mother-in-law fell ill. She had a high fever and couldn't leave her bed. So Jesus went to her, rebuked the fever, and the fever left her. And she immediately got up and served them dinner!

From then on, the ill and infirm flocked to see Jesus. He laid his hands on them and they were healed. "Stay with us!" they begged him. But Jesus said, *I must preach the good news of the kingdom of God to other cities also; for I was sent for this purpose* (4:43).

EVIL SPIRITS

When Satan rebelled against God, some angels followed him and became demons. They are called "evil spirits," and they sometimes torment people. The evil spirits know perfectly well who Jesus is, but they have no power over him. In fact, Jesus chases them away with authority.

THE SYNAGOGUE

Jews gather in the synagogue on the sabbath and on feast days for prayer and readings from Scripture. It's also a place of teaching and preaching. There is hardly any decoration in synagogues, for the Law of Moses forbids paintings and sculptures of most living beings. They are simply furnished: there are benches to sit on and a special cabinet where the scrolls of the Torah are kept.

The Miraculous Catch of Fish

Luke 5:1-11

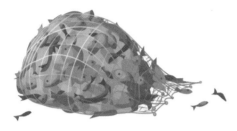

One day, Jesus was walking along the shore of the Sea of Galilee. Many people came to hear him speak. Where could he stand so that everyone could hear him easily? Jesus noticed two boats on the shore beside some **fishermen** washing their nets. Jesus got into one of the boats that belonged to a man called **Simon** and asked him to go out a little way from the shore. Then he sat down and began proclaiming the Good News to the people.

When he finished speaking, he said to Simon, *Put out into the deep and let down your nets for a catch* (5:4). Simon answered, "Master, we worked all night and didn't catch anything! But since it's you who asks, I'll try again."

HARDY FISHERMEN

Fishermen on the Sea of Galilee fished either from the shore, casting circular nets, or in a fishing boat with a square sail. A bit like today's trawlers, the boat would drag behind it a long net. Fishermen had a hard and dangerous trade. They often had to work at night, for that is when fish are most abundant. They had to brave storms at sea. And work wasn't over when they got back to land: then they had to sort the fish, sell them, and care for their nets.

SIMON AND ANDREW

The brothers Simon and Andrew lived in Capernaum near the Sea of Galilee. They were fishermen and owned their own boat. Simon had a fiery temperament; Andrew was more low-key. Andrew had been a disciple of John the Baptist. When John identified Jesus as the Messiah, Andrew decided to follow him. Andrew then introduced Jesus to his brother Simon, who in turn left everything to follow Jesus.

The net filled up with so many fish, it was about to burst! Fortunately, the men in a second boat, including the brothers James and John, came to help them haul it in. No one had ever seen such a catch!

Simon was awestruck. Trembling, he went down on his knees before Jesus, saying, *Depart from me, for I am a sinful man, O Lord* (5:8). But Jesus reassured him, "Do not be afraid; from now on you will be a fisher of men!" After Simon, James, and John rowed the boats back to shore, they left everything and followed Jesus: these were his first ***disciples***.

MASTER AND DISCIPLES

In the time of Jesus, many adults chose to follow a master, or "rabbi," to learn to know God better. They would become his disciples. Disciples had as much respect for their master as for their own parents. What's more, they sometimes even lived with their rabbi for several years. Every disciple chose the master he wished to follow, for there were many rabbis and they didn't always have the same views.

In the Gospels, Jesus is often referred to as "Master" or "Rabbi."

The Healing of a Paralytic

Luke 5:17-26

THE PHARISEES

Religious life was dominated by the Sadducees and the Pharisees. The Sadducees were wealthy and powerful, and they were disliked by the common people. The Pharisees, on the other hand, were often craftsmen or scribes esteemed by all. They were very pious men who knew Jewish Law very well and observed it to the letter.

RISE!

At Mass, we rise to listen to the Gospel. Just as we do to welcome a guest, we stand up as Jesus makes his entry as the Word of God. In the Gospels, he speaks to us. And the healing power of his living Word makes us rise, just like the paralytic.

As Jesus was teaching inside a house, some men brought a paralyzed man on a stretcher. But the crowd was so big that the door was blocked. So the men went up to the roof with their stretcher, removed some tiles, and lowered the stretcher down in front of Jesus. On seeing their faith, Jesus said to the paralytic, *Your sins are forgiven* (5:20).

The scribes and the **Pharisees** took offense at this: "That's blasphemy! Only God can forgive sins!" But Jesus said to them, "Which is easier to say: 'Your sins are forgiven' or 'Rise and walk'? So that you may know that God has given me the authority to forgive sins, I say to this man, 'Rise, take up your strether, and go home.'"

The man immediately got up, picked up his stretcher, and went home glorifying God!

The Twelve Apostles

Luke 6:12-16

Crowds followed Jesus wherever he went, listening to him speak and begging him to heal the sick. But after he healed a man on the sabbath, some scribes and Pharisees were furious with him, thinking that he had disrespected the Law of God.

Among those who followed him, his disciples, Jesus chose twelve men to become his faithful companions, the twelve Apostles: Simon, whom he called Peter, and his brother Andrew, the brothers James and John, Philip, Bartholomew, Matthew, Thomas, James the son of Alphaeus, Simon who was called the Zealot, Jude the son of James, and Judas Iscariot, who became a traitor.

FOLLOWING JESUS

Jesus chose twelve "Apostles," which means "those sent." The Bible tells us little about them. Simon Peter, Andrew, James, and John made a living as fishermen. Matthew was a tax collector. Simon was a "Zealot," a fierce opponent of the Romans. Jude served as a steward.

These simple men, some of them social outcasts, were all very different from one another. Yet Jesus called each of them by name to preach the Gospel to all people.

Andrew

Philip

Simon Peter

Jude

Bartholomew

Matthew

Jesus

John

James

Simon the Zealot

James the son of Alphaeus

Thomas

Judas Iscariot

The Beatitudes

Luke 6:17-37

SATISFIED

Blessed are we when we seek Jesus and hunger for him. He gives us his Word, which is true nourishment to guide our lives. He also gives us his Body and Blood, his divine life, in the Eucharist so that we might become sons and daughters of God. Just as food is necessary for our bodies, Jesus, the Bread of Life, is necessary for our souls. When we receive Communion, Jesus fills us with his love and we hunger no more.

MERCIFUL

The word "merciful" comes from the Latin *misericordia*, which literally means "compassion of the heart." God's mercy is infinite. When we sin, the Lord's heart aches and he is always ready to forgive us. But God is not content just to raise us up when we fall; he also counsels us in order to avoid a fall. So being merciful means to forgive and to accompany others with love.

The crowds following Jesus grew and grew. He looked at these men and women who had come from all over Judea and said to them:

> *Blessed are you poor, for yours*
> *is the kingdom of God.*
> *Blessed are you that hunger now,*
> *for you shall be **satisfied**.*
> *Blessed are you that weep now,*
> *for you shall laugh* (6:20-21).

Blessed are you when people hate you because of me.

Rejoice and be glad for your reward is great in heaven.

Jesus continued his sermon, calling on his followers to love as God the Father loves.

"Do unto others what you would have them do to you," he said.

> *Be **merciful**, even as your Father is merciful. Judge not, and you will not be judged; condemn not, and you will not be condemned; forgive, and you will be forgiven* (6:36).

The House Built upon Rock

Luke 6:46-49

Jesus warned the crowd about those who listen to him but don't put his words into practice: "Everyone who comes to me and hears my words and acts on them is like a wise man building a house. He digs deep and lays the **foundation** upon rock. Then when the rain falls, and the flood rises, his well-built house stands firm. But he who hears my words and does not change his behavior is like the foolish man who builds his house on sand. When the storms come, his house will collapse."

"Foundation"

For a house to remain standing, it needs a good foundation, with footings dug deep into the ground. Foundations make a house solid and able to resist bad weather (heavy rains, strong winds, etc.).

INSIDE A HOUSE

In the time of Jesus, most people lived in simple houses: large, windowless blocks with just the sunlight let in through the door. They were made of mud or sometimes of bricks. There was just one room in which to sleep, cook, eat, and work. Wealthy people had stone houses with an interior courtyard and sometimes more than one story. The rooms were small, and, when it was very hot, people sometime chose to sleep on the roof.

The Centurion's Faith

Luke 7:1-10

Back in Capernaum, Jesus was apporached by some Jewish friends of the Roman **centurion** who had built their synagogue. The centurion's slave was sick and at the point of death. "Would Jesus heal him?" they asked.

Jesus agreed, but as he was approaching the man's house, the centurion sent another friend with this message:

"Lord, do not trouble yourself, for I am not worthy that you should enter under my roof. That is why I didn't presume to come to you myself. But only say the word and my servant shall be healed."

On hearing this, Jesus marveled; he turned to the crowd following him and said, *I tell you, not even in Israel have I found such faith* (7:9).

When the messengers returned to the centurion's house, they found the slave well again.

A Son Restored to His Mother

Luke 7:11-17

Jesus went to the city of Nain. His disciples and a great crowd were traveling with him. Just as he was arriving near the gate of the city, the body of a man was being carried out for burial. He was the only son of a widowed mother. A large crowd of people from the city was with her.

On seeing her, the Lord was filled with compassion and said to her, *Do not weep* (7:13). He went up to the coffin and touched it. The coffin-bearers stopped, and Jesus said, *Young man, I say to you, arise* (7:14). With that, the dead man sat up and began to speak. And Jesus restored him to his mother. **Fear** seized them all; and they glorified God, saying, *A great prophet has arisen among us!* And they also said, *God has visited his people!* (7:16).

TO FEAR GOD?

To fear God is not to be scared of him. Those who fear God simply recognize that God is the all-powerful Creator and that they are very humble compared to him. They are filled with deep respect. The fear of God is one of the seven gifts of the Holy Spirit: it fills us with great awe before the majesty of God and the grandeur of his love.

The Sinful Woman Forgiven

Luke 7:36-50

PRECIOUS PERFUME

Perfume was made by perfumers or, when it was to be burned in the Temple, by priests. People perfumed their homes, their hair, their clothing, and their bodies. During a meal, the master of the house would sometimes perfume the head of one of his guests as a mark of honor. Here, the woman doesn't just pour a little perfume on Jesus' hair; she empties the whole flask over his feet. And it was very expensive perfume! This woman had understood: God's forgiveness is a treasure worth more than all the perfume in the world.

One day, a Pharisee invited Jesus to dine at his home. A woman slipped into the house even though people scorned her because of her bad behavior. She so wanted to meet Jesus. She knelt down before him, weeping. She wetted Jesus' feet with her tears, wiped them with her long hair, kissed them, and poured costly **perfume** over them.

The Pharisee was shocked! He said to himself, "I thought this Jesus might be a prophet, but now I know he can't be. If he were, he would have known this woman is sinful and wouldn't have let her touch him."

Jesus then turned to the Pharisee and said, "I will tell you a **parable**. Two men owed money to a banker. The first one owed five hundred pieces of silver, and the second owed fifty. When they could not pay him back, the banker canceled both their debts. Which of the two men do you think loved the banker more?" The Pharisee replied, "The one who owed him the most, I suppose." Jesus said to him, "Correct."

Then he pointed to the woman at his feet: "Look at this woman! As I came in, you did not embrace me or wash my feet or anoint my head, while she has wiped my feet with her tears and hair. She has covered them with kisses and anointed them with perfume. So I tell you, her sins, which are many, are forgiven, for her heart is full of love; but he who is forgiven little, loves little."

Then Jesus said to the woman, *Your sins are forgiven. Your faith has saved you; go in peace* (7:48, 50). The other guests were greatly surprised and said among themselves, *Who is this, who even forgives sins?* (7:49).

THE PARABLES

The parables are little stories drawn from daily life that help us to understand important things about God. Like most rabbis of his time, Jesus relied on parables to explain, in a colorful yet concrete way, aspects of God and his Kingdom.

The Parable of the Sower

Luke 8:4-15

Jesus told another parable:

"A farmer went out to sow seed. Some seed fell by the roadside, and birds came and gobbled it up. Some fell on rocks. It sprouted right away, but withered because it lacked water. And some fell among thorns that choked it. Finally, some fell into good soil and grew and produced much fruit."

Since his disciples didn't understand, Jesus went on:

"*The seed is the word of God* (8:11). The ones along the roadside are those who hear the Word, but the devil comes and plucks it out of their hearts, so that they believe no more. And the ones among the rocks are those who receive the Word with joy, but they have no roots: their faith doesn't last. Those that fall among the thorns are those who let themselves get tangled in worries or riches. And those that fall in good soil, they are the ones who hear the Word and keep it in a good and generous heart, and bear fruit through perseverance."

HOW TO HEAR THE WORD

Jesus tells his disciples that they must not keep the Word of God to themselves. The Word is like a lamp that must be placed on a lampstand so that it may shine, and others may see the light. As he was speaking, Jesus' mother and brothers (or cousins) asked to see him. But Jesus replied that his mother and his brothers were already there before him: *My mother and my brothers are those who hear the Word of God and do it* (8:21).

The Calming of a Storm at Sea

Luke 8:22-25

The wind was rising. The waters of the lake were becoming rougher and rougher, tossing the boat with Jesus and his disciples. It was a storm. And yet Jesus went on sleeping! Terrified, the disciples shook him: "Master, wake up! We're going to die!" Jesus woke up and rebuked the wind and the raging waves. With that the storm stopped! "Where is your faith?" Jesus asked his friends.

The disciples were amazed. They looked at one another, saying, *Who then is this, that he commands even wind and water, and they obey him?* (8:25).

AN INLAND SEA

Lake Tiberias, also known as the Sea of Galilee, takes two hours to row across. It is renowned for its abundant fish. Its banks are lush and green, and the climate is mild, but there are lots of mosquitoes. Huge storms can suddenly break out then stop just as quickly. The mountains surrounding the lake form a kind of funnel into which the high winds flow, gather strength, and then blow so hard they stir up great waves.

The Raising of the Daughter of Jairus

Luke 8:40-56

Jairus, the ruler of the synagogue, had been on the lookout for Jesus' return to Galilee. When he arrived, he begged him to heal his only daughter, who was dying. As they were on their way to Jairus' house, alas, a messenger arrived to tell them that the child had already died. But Jesus said, *Do not fear; only believe, and she shall be well* (8:50). As he entered the house, he added, *Do not weep; for she is not dead but sleeping* (8:52).

Jesus took the little girl's hand and said in a firm voice, *Child, arise!* (8:54).

At that very moment, she opened her eyes. Jesus ordered that she be given something to eat, and he instructed her parents to tell no one what had happened.

The Twelve Sent Out on Mission

Luke 9:1-6

Jesus gathered together his twelve Apostles. It was time for them to set out on their mission. Jesus gave them the power to command demons, to chase away evil spirits, and to heal the sick and infirm. He sent them out onto the roads of Galilee to proclaim the Kingdom of God.

He said to them, *Take nothing for your journey, no staff, nor bag, nor bread, nor money; and do not have two tunics. And whatever house you enter, stay there, and from there depart. And wherever they do not receive you, when you leave that town shake off the dust from your feet as a testimony against them* (9:3-5).

So the Apostles left, and went from village to village and from house to house. They stayed wherever they were welcomed but kept away from places where they weren't. They went about everywhere proclaiming the Good News and healing the afflicted.

ON THE ROADS OF GALILEE

Jesus sent his disciples out into Galilee. This is a very pleasant region with a mild climate and rich and varied vegetation. The soil is fertile. There are fields, vineyards, and orchards almost everywhere. Every parcel of land is cultivated. There were more than two hundred villages in this small territory, and some fortified cities. Villages were often built on hilltops. The houses were earthen and very simple. The whole village would be centered around the marketplace, with a few workshops and stores, a synagogue, and a well. The people worked in farming or as craftsmen. The language spoken was Aramaic.

Jesus Feeds the Five Thousand

Luke 9:10-17

FIVE LOAVES AND TWO FISH

Jesus fed a crowd of more than five thousand men with just five loaves and two fish! What's more, when everyone had eaten their fill, there were twelve baskets of leftovers, for God always provides more than we ask for. In this episode of the multiplication of the loaves, we recognize certain gestures from the Mass: Jesus takes bread, blesses it, and gives it to his Apostles. At Mass, the priest takes the place of Jesus, and the bread he gives us —transformed into the Body of Christ—feeds our hearts in abundance.

When the Apostles returned from their mission, they couldn't wait to tell Jesus all that had happened! But a crowd followed them, and it was almost nightfall. The Apostles were worried: "Send the crowd away to the villages and countryside so they can find something to eat and somewhere to spend the night, for there's nothing here in this deserted place."

But Jesus said to them, "Give them something to eat yourselves."

"But that's impossible!" they replied with surprise. "We have nothing but five loaves of bread and two fish!" And there were about five thousand men.

Jesus then said, "Have them sit down in groups of fifty." *And taking the five loaves and the two fish he looked up to heaven, and blessed and broke them, and gave them to the disciples to set before the crowd* (9:16).

That day, everyone ate their fill. And when they gathered up what was left over, they had twelve baskets full!

Peter Recognizes Jesus as the Messiah

Luke 9:18-22

TAKING UP ONE'S CROSS AND FOLLOWING JESUS

Jesus explained to his disciples how to follow in his footsteps. To do so, they must forget about themselves. They must be prepared to accept sacrifices and hardships. Jesus offered them a demanding road through life: *If any man would come after me, let him deny himself and take up his cross daily and follow me. For whoever would save his life will lose it; and whoever loses his life for my sake, he will save it* (9:23-24).

As time went by, the crowds were talking about Jesus more and more. Everyone had an opinion about who he was. Jesus asked his disciples about this: "Who do people say that I am?"

The Apostles conferred. It was difficult to give a straight answer. "Some say John the Baptist," they replied. "But others say Elijah. And still others say that you are one of the old prophets who has returned."

Then Jesus asked them, "But who do you say that I am?" Peter immediately spoke up and said, "The Christ, God's Messiah."

Jesus firmly forbade them from repeating this to anyone else. Then he spoke to his disciples of events to come: *The Son of man must suffer many things, and be rejected by the elders and chief priests and scribes, and be killed, and on the third day be raised* (9:22).

The Transfiguration

Luke 9:28-36

One day, Jesus took Peter, John, and James up a mountain to pray. While he was praying, his face changed, and his clothing became dazzling white. He was transfigured.

And behold, two men were with him: **Moses** and **Elijah**! They were speaking about his "exodus," about his going up to Jerusalem.

When Peter saw Jesus appear in his glory, he blurted out, "Master, it is good that we are here! Let us make three tents, one for you and one for Moses and one for Elijah." But no sooner had he spoken than a cloud came and overshadowed them. And from the cloud, a voice could be heard, saying, *This is my Son, my Chosen; listen to him!* (9:35).

WHY MOSES AND ELIJAH?

It's no coincidence that Jesus was transfigured in the presence of Moses and Elijah. These two men both encountered the Lord on Mount Sinai. Moses represents the Law of God, which he received on Mount Sinai and which regulates the life of every Jew. For his part, Elijah represents all the prophets who foretold the coming of the Savior. Above all, it is he who, according to tradition, was to return to make the Messiah known to mankind. So, through their presence with Jesus, Moses and Elijah show that the Law and all the prophets had been fulfilled in the person of Jesus.

THE JEWISH RELIGION

THE LAW OF MOSES

GOD'S COMMANDMENTS

Jewish life is regulated by 613 *mitzvot*, or divine commandments, all drawn from the Torah. The *mitzvot* govern life down to the smallest details: food, family relationships, public life, prayer, religious practice, clothing, and hygiene. Often, however, their interpretation gave rise to disputes between doctors of the Law.

The faithful Jews in the time of Jesus were very attached to all these rules handed down to them by God through Moses. For Jews, respect for the rules meant faithfulness to God's covenant with his people.

THE SABBATH, THE PRIMARY OBLIGATION

The Law entails numerous rituals, of which the most important is respect for the sabbath, the day of rest. On that day, one could not sow seeds, plow, knead dough, cook, sew, write, or even transport an object from one place to another.

The sabbath begins on Friday evening, when a candle is lit, and blessings are said over the light, the wine, and the bread for the meal. The next day, people go to the synagogue to listen to a reading from the Torah and a commentary on it. The sabbath ends that evening with a supper and further blessings. Then normal life resumes.

TO EACH HIS OWN PRACTICE

Jews practice the Law to different degrees of strictness. The rich Sadducees rejected all interpretations of the Law. The Pharisees, on the contrary, never stopped picking over it to better understand it. They held closely to its precepts. But without doubt the most zealous were the Essenes, who lived austerely and withdrew from the world to avoid all temptation.

A WELL-REGULATED LIFE

The life of the believer is marked out in major stages. At eight days old, a baby boy receives his name and is circumcised. One month later, his father "ransoms" him in the Temple. At thirteen, he makes his *bar mitzvah*, that is, his entry into religious adulthood (for girls, it's called a *bat mitzvah*). From then on, he must observe the *mitzvot*. Each stage in the life of a believer enters him deeper into the covenant and unites him a little closer to God.

AND HOW DOES JESUS FIT INTO ALL THIS?

Like all Jews, Jesus respected the Law, but he didn't abide by all of the Pharisees' interpretations of it. Jesus, the Lord, came to fulfill the Law and to show its meaning through the inseparable commandments: "You shall love the Lord your God" and "You shall love your neighbor as yourself." To this Jesus added, "Love one another as I have loved you."

A THOUSAND-YEAR HISTORY

The history of the Jerusalem Temple is long and eventful. King Solomon had the first Temple built in the 10th century B.C. to house the ark of the covenant, which contained the tablets of the Law. But in 587 B.C., the Babylonian King Nebuchadnezzar had it completely demolished and sent the Jewish people into exile. On their return seventy years later, the people quickly rebuilt it. Even though the ark of the covenant had disappeared, the Jews still considered the site of the old Temple as the dwelling place of God. Much later, Herod the Great expanded and greatly embellished the Temple. That was the Temple that Jesus knew.

AT THE HEART OF RELIGIOUS LIFE

The Temple was the physical sign of the presence of God. It was the uncontested center of the Jewish religion, the place where the priests offered sacrifices to God according to the Law of Moses. For the great Jewish festivals, crowds flocked there on pilgrimage from all over the country. These festivals, or feasts, included **Passover**, which commemorates the flight from Egypt, **Pentecost**, which celebrates the receiving of the Law and the earth's fruitfulness; and the Feast of **Tabernacles**, which recalls their life in the wilderness.

THE COURT OF THE PRIESTS

Priests gathered here to offer animal sacrifices on the altar, but also to debate. The fire for the holocausts was kept permanently burning.

THE HOLY OF HOLIES

The sanctuary housed a room called the Holy of Holies. It was God's dwelling place. No one could enter it except the high priest, once a year, on the Day of Atonement (*Yom Kippur*).

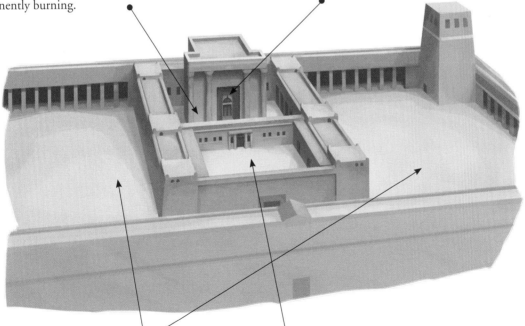

THE COURT OF THE GENTILES

This was the only area open to everyone, Jews and pagans alike. It resembled a big marketplace. Merchants set up shop there, which aroused Jesus' anger.

THE COURT OF THE WOMEN

It wasn't exclusively reserved for women, but as they were forbidden to enter any further into the Temple, it was here that women would carry out their religious obligations.

Jesus
Goes Up to Jerusalem

After all of these events that took place in Galilee, Jesus openly set out on the road to Jerusalem. It's a very long journey when traveling on foot. Along the way, he had numerous encounters and performed many healings. He proclaimed the Good News of the Kingdom of God, and, above all, he explained how to follow him.

The Mission of the Seventy

Luke 10:1-24

FOLLOWING JESUS

Jesus tested those who offered to follow him. When they said they wanted first to go bury their dead or to say goodbye to their families, he challenged them to be with him fully and immediately, and not to worry about what they were leaving behind. *No one who puts his hand to the plow and looks back is fit for the kingdom of God* (9:62).

Jesus chose seventy other disciples and sent them out on the road, two by two.

"Go!" Jesus told them, *The harvest is plentiful, but the laborers are few; pray therefore the Lord of the harvest to send out laborers* (10:2). He instructed them to enter the houses of peace-loving people, to eat and drink whatever they offered, and to heal their sick. "Tell them that the Kingdom of God is near," Jesus said. Then he added, *He who hears you hears me, and he who rejects you rejects me, and he who rejects me rejects him who sent me* (10:16).

When the seventy returned, they rejoiced at being able to cast out demons and to heal the sick in the name of Jesus. And Jesus said to them, *Blessed are the eyes which see what you see!* (10:23).

The Good Samaritan

Luke 10:25-37

One day, a doctor of the Law asked Jesus a question: "Teacher, the Law says we must love our neighbor. But who is my neighbor?"

Jesus then told him this story:

"A man was going down from Jerusalem to Jericho when he was attacked by bandits who beat him up and left him half dead. A priest came down that road; he saw the injured man, but he passed by on the other side. Then a **Levite** came by. He saw the man, but he too passed by on the other side.

"Finally, a Samaritan came by; he saw the wounded man and took pity on him. He went to him and bound up his wounds and took him to an inn. The next day he gave two coins to the innkeeper, saying, 'Take care of him; and whatever more you spend, I will repay you when I come back.'

"Which of these three, do you think, was a neighbor to the injured man?"

The doctor of the Law replied, "The one who showed him mercy."

"You have answered correctly," Jesus told him. "Go and do likewise."

THE LEVITES

As their name suggests, the Levites were the descendants of Levi, one of the twelve sons of Jacob. They worked in the Temple, but they weren't priests: that was a role reserved to the descendants of Aaron. The Levites were more like assistants: they looked after the security of the Temple and prepared the sacrifices and ceremonies; they were in charge of the music and singing; and they collected the tithe, the tax to provide for the priests' upkeep.

Martha and Mary

Luke 10:38-42

As Jesus and his disciples continued on their way, they were invited to the house of two sisters, Martha and Mary. Mary sat at Jesus' feet, attentively listening to him speak. In the meantime, Martha was rushing about preparing the meal. Annoyed at being left to do all the work, Martha finally said to Jesus, "Lord, doesn't it bother you that my sister isn't helping me? She's left me to do everything on my own!" But Jesus replied, *Martha, Martha, you are anxious and troubled about many things; one thing is needful. Mary has chosen the good portion, which shall not be taken away from her* (10:41-42).

The Our Father

Luke 11:1-30

The disciples wanted to pray like Jesus. So they asked him, *Lord, teach us to pray* (11:1). And Jesus taught them this prayer:

Our Father, who art in heaven,
hallowed be thy name;
thy kingdom come,
thy will be done
on earth as it is in heaven.
Give us this day our daily bread,
and forgive us our trespasses,
as we forgive those who trespass against us;
and lead us not into temptation,
but deliver us from evil.

Then he added, *Ask, and it will be given you; seek and you will find; knock, and it will be opened to you. ...How much more will the heavenly Father give the Holy Spirit to those who ask him!* (11:9-13).

PROVIDENCE

Jesus encouraged his disciples not to worry about material things that come and go, but instead to trust in God's care.

"Look at the ravens," he said. "They don't plant or harvest; they have no barn or storehouse, yet God feeds them. And how much more valuable you are than the birds! So don't seek for what you are to eat or drink, and don't fret. Seek instead the treasure that never loses its value, that no thief can take from you. *For where your treasure is, there will your heart be also*" (12:34).

The Crippled Woman

Luke 13:10-17

JESUS HEALS

The sick, the crippled, the blind, the lepers—they all came to Jesus in the hope that he would cure them. And Jesus certainly healed hundreds of them. The Gospels recount many times when Jesus healed not just the body but also the soul. These miraculously healed people whose sins were forgiven came into direct contact with God's immense love for them. Now that truly was the start of new life!

It was the sabbath day and Jesus was teaching in the synagogue. Among the people listening to him was a woman who was bent over. She was completely unable to stand up straight, and she had been living like that for eighteen years! Jesus decided he must do something for her. He said to her, *Woman, you are freed from your infirmity* (13:12). And at that very moment, she was healed: she stood up as straight as an arrow! She was delighted and praised God. But the head of the synagogue was not pleased and said, "This is the sabbath day, when work is forbidden! Those who wish to be healed have only to come back another day!" This angered Jesus, who replied, "You've understood nothing! Don't you give your donkey something to eat and drink even on the sabbath? This woman is worth much more than any animal! She's been suffering for eighteen years already and shouldn't have to wait a day longer to be healed!" The head of the synagogue was embarrassed, and everyone else rejoiced at the wonderful things Jesus was doing.

The Parables of the Mustard Seed and the Yeast

Luke 13:18-21

Jesus spoke to his disciples in parables to help them understand what the **Kingdom of God** was like. "What can I compare it to?" he said. "It's like a tiny little mustard seed that a man planted in his garden. It grew into a great big tree, and the birds came and made their nests in its branches."

Then Jesus gave another example: "To what shall I compare the Kingdom of God? It is like yeast that a woman took and mixed with three measures of flour until the whole batch of dough had risen."

WHEN WILL THE KINGDOM COME?

Jesus spoke of the nearness of the Kingdom of God. The Jews of that period understood this to mean that God would soon arrive to reign over them. But Jesus reveals that the Kingdom of God is already at work within us. It is like the invisible yeast in the dough that makes it rise little by little. We must cooperate with it and follow Jesus more and more. His Kingdom is so precious that his followers are willing to give up anything for it.

Choosing the Lowest Place

Luke 14:7-11

LET THE FEAST BEGIN!

The Jews hosted guests often and generously. Family, friends, mere acquaintances— everyone was welcome. The banquet would be held outdoors, in the courtyard of the house. Food and wine were served in abundance. The guests wore party outfits. Upon arrival, everyone would wash their feet and their right hands, the hands they would eat with. The master of the house would anoint the head of the most important guest with perfume, bless the table, and then take charge of serving the meal.

Jesus was invited to dinner at the home of a Pharisee. Noticing guests who were trying to sit in places of honor, he said:

"When someone invites you to a wedding banquet, don't sit down in the seat of honor, in case someone more distinguished than you has been invited, and the host comes and says to you, 'Give your place to this person.' Then, with great embarrassment, you will take the lowest place. Instead, when you are invited, go and sit in the lowest place, so that, when your host comes, he may say to you, 'My friend, move up to a higher position.' *For every one who exalts himself will be humbled, and he who humbles himself will be exalted*" (14:11).

Invite the Poor

Luke 14:12-24

Then Jesus said to the host who had invited him:

"When you hold a lunch or a dinner, don't invite your friends or your relatives or your rich neighbors; they may invite you in return, and you will be repaid. Instead, when you hold a banquet, invite the poor, the crippled, the lame, the blind, and you will be blessed, because they have nothing to give you in return. You will be repaid by God."

Then, speaking to all the guests, Jesus added:

"A man gave a great banquet, but, when the meal was ready, all those invited made excuses, and no one came. In anger, the master of the house told his servant, 'Hurry out into the city streets, and bring back the poor and maimed and blind and lame. *For I tell you, none of those men who were invited shall taste my banquet*'" (14:24).

JESUS AND THE POOR

The poor held a very special place in Jesus' heart—not only those short of money, but also those who were sick or looked down upon because their sins were obvious. Jesus knew that those who have the greatest need for God often accept God's message more willingly. To get close to Jesus, let us too be "poor"! Let's not be too attached to our possessions, and let's admit that we're not perfect.

The Lost Sheep

Luke 15:1-7

THE SHEPHERD

The image of the shepherd had already figured in the Old Testament. When Ezekiel rebuked the leaders of the Jewish people for not resisting the spread of false beliefs, he said they were behaving like bad shepherds who didn't guide their flocks well.

Ezekiel foretold that God would send a shepherd who would care for his people. That good shepherd is Jesus.

PRAYER
Psalm 23:1-3

The Lord is my shepherd,
I shall not want;
he makes me lie down
in green pastures.
He leads me beside
still waters;
he restores my soul.
He leads me in paths
of righteousness
for his name's sake.

Among the people who came to listen to Jesus, many were not very faithful to the Law of Moses; people called them "sinners." The priests and the scribes were shocked that Jesus welcomed them. So Jesus told them this story:

"If one of you had a hundred sheep and lost one of them, wouldn't you leave the ninety-nine to go looking for the lost sheep? And when you found it, you would carry it home on your shoulders rejoicing and calling to your friends and neighbors: 'Look! I've found the sheep that was lost!'"

There will be more joy in heaven over one sinner who repents than over ninety-nine righteous persons who need no repentance (15:7).

The Prodigal Son

Luke 15:11-32

Jesus told another story:

"A man had two sons. One day, the younger said to him, 'Dad, give me my share of my inheritance now.' Then he left for a faraway land, where he squandered his whole fortune in wild living. He hadn't a penny left to his name. To earn a little money, he tended someone's pigs. He was so hungry he would have gladly eaten the slop given to the animals! In despair, he said to himself, 'My father's servants eat bread every day while here am I, dying of hunger! I will go home to my father and I will tell him that I am not worthy to be his son, that he should treat me like a servant.'

"So he returned to his father's house. While he was still a long way off, his father caught sight of him; he ran to him, took him in his arms, and covered him with kisses. His son said to him, 'Father, what I did was very wrong. I am no longer worthy to be called your son.'

SERVANTS OF THE WEALTHY

The wealthiest people had many servants living in their homes. Female servants cleaned, cooked, fetched water, spun wool, and wove cloth. The male servants more often worked in the fields. The Law of Moses required that a master treat his servants very well, like his own brothers and sisters.

FORGIVEN AND HAPPY!

The parable of the prodigal son shows us just how much the Lord loves us. The father isn't satisfied just to forgive his son when he comes home; he watches for his return each day. And when this well-beloved yet sinful son returns, his father clasps him to his heart, forgives him, and celebrates.

God awaits us, too, hoping that we will ask his forgiveness in the Sacrament of Reconciliation. When we do, there is great celebration in heaven. And the banquet that is Communion becomes even lovelier, because we are very close to God, clasped tightly to his heart.

"But the father said to his servants, 'Quick! Bring him the best robe, and sandals, and a golden ring. Kill the fatted calf. Prepare a great feast, for my son was lost and now he is found!'

"The elder son was coming in from the fields. He heard music and dancing and asked what was happening. A servant told him, 'Your brother has come home, and there's a celebration!' The elder son was furious. He refused to go into the house. He complained to his father, 'I've worked for you for years and I've always obeyed you, but you've never given me even the least little lamb to feast on with my friends! Yet you have the fatted calf killed for that good-for-nothing son of yours who squandered all your money!' Then the father replied, 'My child, you are always with me, and all that is mine is yours. Come celebrate with us; your brother was dead and is alive again!'"

PRAYER
Psalm 51:1-2, 12-13

Have mercy on me, O God,
according to your merciful love;
according to your abundant mercy blot out
my transgressions.

Restore to me the joy of your salvation,
and uphold me with a willing spirit.
Then I will teach transgressors your ways,
and sinners will return to you.

The Pharisee and the Tax Collector

Luke 18:9-14

TAX COLLECTORS

Tax collectors were Jews who gathered taxes for the Romans. They were considered traitors because they worked for the occupiers, and they were suspected of corruptly enriching themselves. What's more, they were despised by pious Jews for handling pagan money.

PRAYER
Psalm 131:1-2

O LORD, my heart
is not lifted up,
my eyes are not raised
too high;
I do not occupy myself
with things
too great and
too marvelous for me.
But I have calmed
and quieted my soul,
like a child quieted at its
mother's breast;
like a child that is quieted
is my soul.

Jesus was speaking to certain people who were convinced of their own righteousness and looked down on others, and he told them this story:

"A Pharisee and a **tax collector** went to pray in the Temple. The Pharisee prayed like this: 'Thank you, God, that I am not like other men. I obey your laws, while they are thieves and liars, like that tax collector!' For his part, the tax collector didn't even dare raise his eyes to heaven. He prayed like this: 'God, be merciful to me, a sinner!' (18:13).

"The tax collector went home forgiven by God, not the Pharisee," Jesus said. *For every one who exalts himself will be humbled, but he who humbles himself will be exalted* (18:14).

Jesus and the Children

Luke 18:15-17

One day, some mothers brought their children to Jesus for him to bless them. That annoyed his disciples, who said, "This is grown-up business! Leave us alone!"

But Jesus scolded them. He called the children over to him and said, *Let the children come to me; for to such belongs the kingdom of God.... Whoever does not receive the kingdom of God like a child shall not enter it* (18:16-17).

CHILDREN AS ROLE MODELS!

When Jesus asked his disciples to be like little children, he was saying something very surprising. At that time, children weren't considered important, and they weren't asked their opinion. Their parents even decided what they would do when they grew up. How does Jesus want us to be like children? By trusting in God, believing that he is our loving Father.

The Rich Young Man

Luke 18:18-30

THE PASSION FORETOLD A THIRD TIME

Gathering the twelve Apostles around him, Jesus said, "Behold, we are going up to Jerusalem, and everything that was written by the prophets will be fulfilled." He then foretold that he would be handed over to the Romans, mocked, scourged, and killed, and then rise from the dead on the third day.

The Apostles listened to Jesus, but they did not understand him.

A rich man asked Jesus, "What must I do to gain eternal life?"

"Do you know the commandments?" Jesus asked him.

"Yes," he said, "I have obeyed them since I was a boy."

Jesus told him, "You still lack one thing: sell all that you have, give it to the poor, and you will have treasure in heaven. Then come follow me." But when the man heard this, he went away sad, for he had many possessions.

Then Jesus said, "There is no one who leaves house or wife or brothers or parents or children for the sake of the Kingdom of God who will not receive much more in this present day, and eternal life in the time to come."

The Healing of the Blind Man of Jericho

Luke 18:35-43

A blind man was sitting by the roadside near Jericho. His eyes had grown dim, but his ears worked just fine! He could hear a commotion and the noise of an approaching crowd.

"What's happening?" he asked, tugging on the robe of a passerby.

"Jesus of Nazareth is coming this way," the man told him. With that, the blind man cried out, *Jesus, Son of David, have mercy on me!* (35:38).

The crowd shoved him away and told him to keep quiet. But he cried out all the more, *Son of David, have mercy on me!* (18:39).

Jesus heard him, stopped, and had the man brought to him.

"What do you want me to do for you?"

He said, "Lord, I want to see again."

And Jesus said to him, "Regain your sight! Your faith has saved you."

And immediately he regained his sight and followed Jesus, glorifying God. On seeing this miracle, the people gave praise to God.

ASK AND YOU SHALL RECEIVE

Jesus heard the blind man by the roadside calling to him. He could have simply walked by and cured him from a distance. But he took the time to stop and ask this man what he wanted. And the blind man's reply was a cry from the heart: "I want to see!" Touched by this man's faith, Jesus restored his sight.

At Mass, let's not hesitate to cry out our own prayer to Jesus. Let's put all our heart and all our faith into it. Jesus is there, listening to each one of us personally. He always answers our prayers in some form or another, even if it's not always quite the way we are expecting.

Jesus Stays at Zacchaeus' House

Luke 19:1-10

As Jesus was passing through the city of Jericho, people came out into the streets to see him. It so happened that a man named Zacchaeus lived there. He was the chief tax collector and a rich man. Since he worked for the Romans, the people hated him. Zacchaeus wanted to see Jesus, but he was too short to see over everyone's heads. Then he had an idea: he ran on ahead, and in the spot where Jesus would pass by, he climbed up a sycamore tree.

When Jesus arrived there, he looked up and said to him, "Zacchaeus, quick, come down; for I must stay at your house today." Zacchaeus hurried down and welcomed Jesus into his home with joy.

On seeing this, the people complained: "He's gone to stay in the house of a sinner!" Zacchaeus then said to Jesus, "Behold, Lord, I will give half of my possessions to the poor; and if I have cheated anyone of anything, I will pay him back four times over." And Jesus said to him, *Today salvation has come to this house, since he also is a son of Abraham. For the **Son of man** came to seek and to save the lost* (19:10).

68

JESUS AND JEWISH SOCIETY

OUTCASTS

PURE OR IMPURE?

Jews strictly adhered to purification rituals and avoided anything that could make them unclean. The Pharisees turned this into a kind of religion within the religion, and they felt superior because they respected Moses' commandments to the letter. In fact, they weren't just content to carry out the purifications carefully laid down by Moses. They analyzed every situation to establish new and ever more complex rules. There are entire volumes setting out what is pure and impure! Jesus sometimes questioned their judgment. Men look only at a person's outward appearance, he said, whereas God sees the heart.

SOCIAL OUTCASTS

For many Jews, illness or handicap didn't happen just by chance. It was considered a punishment for sins commited either by oneself or by one's ancestors. Some sick men and women were excluded from society. They didn't have the right to go to the Temple or to enter public places. Nevertheless, they were given alms (charitable gifts) as the Law requires, on condition that the sick person was Jewish! For a Jew was allowed to give alms only to another Jew.

HATED BY ALL

Tax collectors, agents of the Roman government, were among the most hated people in society. They were considered traitors for working on behalf of the pagan occupier. They were also called thieves because many took advantage of their position to pocket money for themselves. Both Matthew and Zaccheus were tax collectors. The crowd was scandalized that Jesus welcomed them and visited them.

BAD NEIGHBORS

The men and women of Samaria, the region between Judea and Galilee, were despised by the Jews. The Samaritans were distant cousins of the Jews, cut off from Temple Judaism by foreign invasions of Israel. In the time of Jesus, to call someone a Samaritan was the worst of insults!

A HUGE CROWD

Most of those who came to see and hear Jesus are unknown. They were simple, devout Jews who found his words clear and easy to understand, who preferred parables to flowery speeches. Some were social outcasts; others were former disciples of John the Baptist. Jesus attracted the sick in need of healing, the sinners in search of forgiveness, and the poor in want of hope. Some rich and prominent people sought out Jesus. They kept a low profile. They came to Jesus in secret, at night, like Nicodemus, a Pharisee and a leader of the Jews.

THE FAITHFUL AMONG THE FAITHFUL

Jesus was surrounded by crowds wherever he went. Among them most often were his twelve Apostles. When they weren't off on mission, they followed him. Members of his family were with him, too. Mary, his mother, was present, along with some cousins: James, Joseph, Simon, and Jude. Many women followed Jesus: Martha and Mary, the sisters of Jesus' great friend Lazarus; Mary Magdalene, a formerly sinful woman; as well as Joanna, the wife of Herod's steward.

EVEN HIS OPPONENTS FOLLOWED HIM

Among those who followed Jesus were also many grumblers: Pharisees, scribes, doctors of the Law. They were very annoyed by all these crowds following Jesus. They were jealous. They followed Jesus, trying to catch him in a mistake so that they could accuse him of blasphemy. They listened to every word he said, always looking for errors, and asked him questions to trap him. They knew the Law well and were very sure of themselves. Jesus responded to them using their own arguments. He would always quote Holy Scripture so that they couldn't accuse him of any wrong.

The Death of Jesus

Jesus entered Jerusalem knowing he was going to be put to death. What he found there saddened him: the lack of faith, the injustice. He opposed the religious leaders, who paid someone to betray him. He was arrested and falsely accused. His Passion was long and painful. Innocent, he submitted to it all. Faithful to his mission, he went right to the limit of love. He was crucified like a common criminal and died on the cross. But death did not have the last word.

The Entry into Jerusalem

Luke 19:28-44

A CROWD OF PILGRIMS

Who were all these people at the entrance to Jerusalem? They had gathered from all over the land for Passover, because the sacrifice of the Passover lambs took place in the Jerusalem Temple. People came in caravans. They slept in tents on the rooftops of the houses. Passover, which commemorates the escape from Egypt and the freeing of the people of Israel from slavery, lasts a week.

As Jesus drew near to Jerusalem, he instructed his disciples, "Go into the next village. There you will find a tethered donkey, on which no one has ever sat. Untie it and bring it here."

The disciples brought the donkey to Jesus, and he rode it into Jerusalem. Along the way, the crowd spread their cloaks on the ground before him. They hailed him, waving palm branches and shouting, "Blessed is the King who comes in the name of the Lord! Hosanna in the highest!"

When Jesus saw the city, he wept over it, saying, "O Jerusalem! The days will come when your enemies will surround you, and hem you in on every side. They will destroy you, you and your children within you, and they will not leave one stone upon another; because you did not recognize the moment when God visited you."

THE DESTRUCTION OF THE TEMPLE

After the Death of Jesus, there were more and more uprisings of the Jews against the Romans. Even among themselves, they could no longer get along. In A.D. 70, the Romans laid siege to Jerusalem. The city was demolished, and the Temple destroyed, just as Jesus had predicted. Nothing remains of it today but one of the foundation walls.

The Emperor's Tax

Luke 20:20-26

Some were plotting to catch Jesus in a trap. They went to see him and began by flattering him: "Master, we know you always speak the truth. You're not swayed by people of power, and you always teach the true path to God." Then they asked him their question: "Should we pay the tax to the Roman emperor?"

They had him in a corner: If Jesus answered yes, the people would say, "He's just like the tax collectors; he's working for the Romans!" And if he said no, he would be in trouble with the Romans!

Jesus said to them, "Show me a coin." They did as he asked and handed him a coin. Jesus asked them, "Whose image is that on the coin? Whose name is on it?" And they answered, "It's the emperor, Caesar." Then Jesus said to them, *Render to Caesar the things that are Caesar's, and to God the things that are God's* (20:25). And the people who had asked the question were caught in their own trap!

THE TAX PAID TO CAESAR

To show their power over the people, the Roman occupiers exacted taxes from the Jews. There were two kinds of tax, both resented by the people. The tax on lands and inhabitants was paid directly to the emperor's agents. The tax on merchandise was gathered by tax collectors, Jews working for the Romans.

WIDOWS

Among women, widows had the hardest lives. Without the support of their husbands, they had less social status than married women. They often fell into poverty, since it was the man who worked to earn the family's living. Sometimes they were even reduced to begging to survive.

WHY THE COLLECTION

At the Offertory of the Mass, bread and wine is presented to offer up our work and our lives to the Lord. In olden days, this bread and wine was offered by the faithful. Today the parish provides the bread and the wine, but each of us places some of our money in the basket that is passed. This money goes toward supporting the parish and the diocese, to provide for the livelihood of the priests and the whole Church, and to help the very poor.

The Poor and Generous Widow

Luke 21:1-4

Jesus was in the Temple observing the people coming to make their offerings. There were rich people and others more humble. A very poor **widow** came forward. Since her husband had died, she had hardly anything left to live on. Yet, when it was her turn, the woman slipped two little coins into the treasury. On seeing that, Jesus said, "Truly I tell you, this poor widow has put in more than all of them; for they all contributed out of their excess wealth, but she in her poverty has given all she had to live on."

The Last Supper

Luke 22:7-38

Jesus put Peter and John in charge of organizing the Passover meal, which he wished to share with his Apostles.

"Where would you like us to prepare it?" they asked him.

"As you enter the city," he said, "a man carrying a jug of water will meet you. Follow him to the house he enters and tell the owner that the Master asks where the guest room is where he is to share the Passover meal with his disciples. He will show you a large upper room. Prepare our meal there."

THE FEAST OF PASSOVER

Passover is the most important feast in the Jewish religion. It commemorates the Jews' liberation from slavery and their exodus, that is, their flight from Egypt led by Moses. This feast lasts for eight days and begins, on the first evening, with a special meal described in the Book of Exodus. Unleavened bread is eaten with a freshly sacrificed lamb. It was during this meal that Jesus chose to announce his death. He wished in this way to signify that he was fulfilling what had been foretold in the Book of Exodus: the liberation from sin and the entry into new life with God.

THE BETRAYAL OF JUDAS

As the feast of unleavened bread, Passover, approached, Satan entered the heart of Judas Iscariot. Judas was one of Jesus' Apostles, one of the Twelve. He went to the high priests, the scribes, and the captains of the guard who were looking for a way to get rid of Jesus. They offered him money in exchange for his betrayal. Judas agreed, took the money, and began looking for the best moment to hand Jesus over to them.

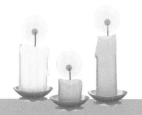

THE MYSTERY OF THE EUCHARIST

The Mass has its origins in Jesus' Last Supper with his disciples, on Holy Thursday. On that day, Jesus established the Eucharist. He took bread, broke it, blessed it, and gave it to his Apostles. And he said to them, "This is my Body; this is my Blood. Do this in memory of me." He charged his Apostles to follow his example by offering his Body and Blood to all men and women, that they might be saved.

When everything was ready, Jesus sat down at table with his Apostles and said to them:

"It was my great desire to eat this last Passover meal with you. For I tell you, I shall not eat it again until it is fulfilled in the Kingdom of God."

And he took bread, and when he had given thanks he broke it and gave it to them, saying, "This is my body which is given for you. Do this in remembrance of me." And likewise the chalice after supper, saying, "This chalice which is poured out for you is the new covenant in my blood.

"But behold the hand of him who betrays me is with me on the table. For the Son of man goes as it has been determined; but woe to that man by whom he is betrayed!" (22:19-22).

The Apostles began murmuring among themselves, wondering who the traitor could possibly be. Then they began arguing with each other about who among them was the greatest.

But Jesus said that they should follow his example by serving one another. *I am among you as one who serves* (22:27).

As the hour approached for Judas to hand him over, Peter swore he would remain loyal to Jesus: *Lord, I am ready to go with you to prison and to death.* But Jesus replied, *I tell you, Peter, the cock will not crow this day, until you three times deny that you know me* (22:33-34).

The Night on the Mount of Olives

Luke 22:39-53

THE GARDEN OF GETHSEMANE

The garden of Gethsemane, on the Mount of Olives, is just outside the walls of Jerusalem. It is planted with trees and linked to the Temple by a bridge. The tombs of many prophets and figures from the Old Testament are found there. There is also an olive press (the meaning of the Hebrew word *gethsemane*). On the evening of Holy Thursday, right after the Passover meal, Jesus went there with his Apostles. Since this was not the first time, Judas would have had no trouble finding him.

As soon as the meal was over, Jesus went with his disciples to the Mount of Olives. He told them, *Pray that you may not enter into temptation* (22:40).

Then he withdrew from them, knelt down, and began to pray:

Father, if you are willing, remove this chalice from me; nevertheless not my will, but yours, be done (22:42).

When he got up, he found his disciples asleep. He said to them, *Why do you sleep? Rise and pray that you may not enter into temptation* (22:46).

At that very moment, a crowd arrived with Judas in the lead. He approached Jesus and kissed him. Jesus said to him, *Would you betray the Son of man with a kiss?* (22:48).

Then Jesus said to those who had come to arrest him, "Have you come with swords and clubs to arrest me like a common thief? I was with you day after day in the Temple, and you didn't stop me."

But the guards seized Jesus and led him off to the high priest.

80

Denied by Peter

Luke 22:54-62

Peter followed the soldiers at a distance as they led Jesus away. He waited outside in front of the house of **Caiaphas** with the servants. A maid looked at him closely and exclaimed, "This man was with Jesus, too!" Peter lied, "No, I don't know him." A little later someone else saw him and said, "You, too, you're one of that man's friends!" But Peter said, "I am not!" An hour later, a third servant insisted, "I'm sure you were with that Jesus; you have a Galilean accent!" Peter replied, "I don't know what you're talking about."

And immediately, while he was still speaking, the cock crowed. And the Lord turned and looked at Peter. And Peter remembered the word of the Lord, how he had said to him, "Before the cock crows today, you will deny me three times." And he went out and wept bitterly (22:60-62).

CAIPHAS AND THE SANHEDRIN

In the time of Jesus, the Sanhedrin was the highest authority on questions of religion. It was comprised of seventy-one members: the high priest (in this case, Caiaphas), priests, scribes, doctors of the Law, and representatives of the most prominent families. The Sanhedrin decided how the Law was to be applied, and judged people who did not obey it. Jesus was led to the house of Caiaphas because his enemies had accused him of blasphemy, of making himself out to be God.

Jesus Mocked and Scorned

Luke 22:63–23:25

Poor Jesus! The guards in charge of him beat him and mocked him. They sent him before Caiaphas, the high priest, then before Pilate, and then before Herod.

"This man is a troublemaker," the crowd said. "He claims he's the king of the Jews."

Pilate asked him, "Are you the king of the Jews?" Jesus replied, "If you say so."

For Pilate, this wasn't enough to label Jesus a criminal. He intended to give him a light punishment and then have him released, but the crowd wouldn't hear of it.

"Put him to death!" they shouted. *Crucify, crucify him!* (23:21).

Pilate feared the crowd. He handed Jesus over to be crucified, since that's what they wanted.

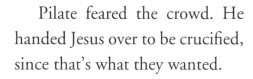

The Crucifixion

Luke 23:26-43

They made Jesus carry his cross to the place where he was to be put to death. The cross was so heavy that the Roman soldiers forced a man named Simon of Cyrene to help Jesus. A great crowd followed them.

At the place called Calvary, Jesus was nailed to the cross between two criminals. Jesus said, *Father, forgive them; for they know not what they do* (23:34). Above Jesus' head, a sign gave the reason for his death sentence: "Jesus of Nazareth, the King of the Jews." Some people sneered, *He saved others; let him save himself, if he is the Christ of God, his Chosen One!* (23:35). One of the two criminals crucified next to Jesus jeered at him, *Are you not the Christ? Save yourself and us!* (23:39).

But the other one said, "Will you mock God right to the end? You and I deserved our punishment, but this man did no wrong." And looking at Jesus he said, *Jesus, remember me when you come into your kingly power* (23:42). And Jesus said to him, *Truly, I say to you, today you will be with me in Paradise* (23:43).

SUCH GREAT LOVE!

Why did Jesus accept all this suffering? He, the Son of God, could easily have escaped it. But, to save mankind from sin, he obeyed the will of his Father and bore the suffering we sinners deserve. *Greater love has no man than this, that a man lay down his life for his friends,* Jesus said (John 15:13). And he didn't just say it, he actually did it. Through love of us, he accepted death on a cross. He knew that only this sacrifice, the greatest of all, could conquer death, deliver us from sin, and bring us back to life with God.

The Death of Jesus
Luke 23:44-49

It was about noon when darkness covered the land. The sun was hidden for three hours. And suddenly, the veil of the Temple was torn in two. *Jesus, crying with a loud voice, said, "Father, into your hands I commit my spirit!"* (23:46).

His head dropped down on his chest. Jesus was dead.

On seeing this, a centurion standing at the foot of the cross praised God and said, *Certainly this man was innocent!* (23:47). The crowd was distraught and returned home beating their breasts in shame, crushed at having condemned an innocent man to death.

THE WONDROUS SIGN OF THE CROSS

The cross, that terrible object of torture and humiliation, was scandalous for the Jews. And yet, for us Christians, it is the symbol of God's love for mankind. It is through the cross that Jesus saved us. When we make the Sign of the Cross, we should do it slowly and with great respect. The Sign of the Cross is also a way of saying that we believe in one God in three Persons: the Father, and the Son, and the Holy Spirit.

The Burial

Luke 23:50-56

The feast of Passover was about to begin. The sabbath rest would start in just a few hours. Jesus had to be taken down from the cross and buried quickly. They couldn't just leave him there like that. It was then that a rich man named Joseph of Arimathea arrived. He had followed Jesus, for he too was awaiting the Kingdom of God. Joseph went to Pilate and asked for Jesus' body, to lay it in a tomb that he owned nearby.

There was no time to lose. They took Jesus' body down from the cross, covered him in a shroud, and placed him in the tomb carved out of the rock, a brand-new tomb in which no one had yet been buried.

From a distance, the women who had followed Jesus watched what they did. They noted where the body of the Lord was laid. For as soon as the sabbath rest was over, they intended to return with spices and perfumes to anoint his body.

THE TOMB

In the time of Jesus, Jewish tombs were carved into the rock, like caves. A large stone was rolled in front to close off the entrance. The body was laid on a ledge carved into the wall. Normally, there would be several ledges, so that the tomb could be used for several people, for example, from the same family.

BURYING THE DEAD

At the time of Jesus, as soon as someone died, the body was washed and then rubbed with perfumed oils. It was then wrapped in a shroud. The face was first covered with a cloth and the hands bound in strips of linen. Then the body was placed in the ground in a common grave. Only the wealthy had tombs carved into rock and closed off with a large stone.

The Resurrection of Jesus

Women were the first to make the incredible discovery: the tomb was empty! The Lord had risen, just as he had said. The disciples ran one after the other to see for themselves. The Risen One met them, appeared to them, spoke to them, and sent them out to witness to all they had seen and heard. Then he disappeared from their sight: he rose into heaven at his Ascension. It was now up to the disciples to spread the Good News!

The Women at the Tomb

Luke 24:1-12

MARY MAGDALENE

Mary Magdalene's name comes from the town where she was born, Magdala, on the shores of the Sea of Galilee. Mary Magdalene had followed Jesus ever since the day he cured her. She was present at the foot of the cross with Mary, his mother. According to John the Evangelist, she was the first person to see the risen Jesus, and she announced the news to the Apostles.

As soon as the sabbath was over, Mary Magdalene and some other women returned to the tomb. The stone had already been rolled away to one side. And the body of Jesus was gone! Two angels appeared to them and said, *Why do you seek the living among the dead? He is not here, but has risen. Remember how he told you, while he was still in Galilee, that the Son of man must be delivered into the hands of sinful men, and be crucified, and on the third day rise* (24:5-7).

When the women reported these words to the Apostles, they didn't believe them. But when Peter ran to the tomb, he found it empty!

The Disciples
of Emmaus

Luke 24:13-35

On the evening of the first day of the week, the day the tomb was found empty, two of Jesus' disciples left Jerusalem to walk to a village called Emmaus. Jesus himself met them along the way, but the disciples were unable to recognize him; they thought he was just another traveler like them.

Jesus said to them, "What were you talking about as you walked along? You look so sad!" One of the disciples answered, "And with good reason! Are you the only person who hasn't heard about the things that happened in Jerusalem a few days ago?"

"What things?" Jesus asked.

The disciples explained: "Jesus of Nazareth was a great prophet, but our religious leaders condemned him to death and had him crucified. And we had been hoping he would be the liberator of the people of Israel! Now, on the third day, we've been told something incredible. It seems some women from our group went to the tomb this morning and found it empty. They said that angels told them he's alive! But no one has seen Jesus himself."

TRAVELING IN PALESTINE

In the time of Jesus, people didn't go sightseeing. They traveled only for business, family matters, or religious observances. The wealthiest would travel on horseback; everyone else went on foot. The main roads were paved. A traveler journeying on foot would carry his money in a money-belt tied firmly around his waist. He often took an extra pair of sandals and a tunic, not forgetting a sack for his food. Travelers would lodge along the way with locals, who readily welcomed them.

A SUFFERING MESSIAH

In the time of Jesus, many Jews hoped for a Messiah who would be a great military leader to chase the Romans out by force. But Jesus reminded the disciples on the way to Emmaus that certain prophets had foretold a very different kind of Messiah: a humble Messiah who would save mankind through his suffering. The prophet Isaiah spoke this way about the mysterious "servant of God," who would be hated by all and put to death. He prophesied that this servant would triumph and be rewarded by God.

Jesus replied, "You really haven't understood anything! How hard you find it to believe what's written in the Scriptures! For didn't the prophets say it was necessary for the Messiah to suffer in order to enter into his glory?"

And Jesus went back over all the texts of the Bible that spoke of him.

They were now close to Emmaus. Jesus seemed about to continue on his way, but the disciples begged him, "Please, come stay with us; it's getting late and will soon be dark." And Jesus accepted.

When he was at table with them, he took the bread and blessed and broke it, and gave it to them. And their eyes were opened and they recognized him (24:30-31).

And with that, he vanished from sight! They said to each other, "Weren't our hearts burning within us while he talked to us on the road and explained the Scriptures to us?" They got up right away and hurried back to Jerusalem. There they found the eleven Apostles gathered together, and they said, "The Lord has risen indeed, and has appeared to Simon Peter!" Then the two disciples told what had happened on the road, and how Jesus was made known to them in the breaking of the bread.

Jesus Appears to the Apostles

Luke 24:36-49

THE SIGN OF PEACE

"Peace to you!" These were Jesus' first words to his Apostles after the Resurrection. He showed them his wounds to prove that he was not a ghost but truly risen from the dead, and he calmed their fears. But this peace goes much further than that. Through his Resurrection, Jesus offers us the promise of eternal life, of victory over sin and death. These words that we repeat at Mass should fill us with hope.

The Apostles were gathered together. They could hardly believe the things that had been happening. While they were speaking, Jesus was suddenly there among them. He said to them, *Peace to you* (24:36).

The Apostles were terrified. Were they seeing a ghost? But Jesus went on, "Why are you frightened, and why are there doubts in your hearts? Look at my hands and my feet: it's me! Touch me, look! A ghost doesn't have flesh and bones as you see that I have." And he showed them his hands and his feet.

Then he asked for something to eat while he explained the Scriptures to them:

"It was written that the Christ would suffer and rise from the dead on the third day. You are witnesses of these things. For my part, I am going to send you what my Father promised. As for you, stay in the city until you are clothed with power from on high."

The Ascension

Luke 24:50-53

After their meal, Jesus led his disciples outside the city. They went together to a place called Bethany. There Jesus raised his hands and blessed them. *While he blessed them, he parted from them, and was carried up into heaven* (24:51).

The Apostles bowed down in worship of the Lord Jesus. Soon they could see him no more. He had disappeared.

Then, without a moment's hesitation, they returned to Jerusalem as Jesus had told them to do. Their hearts were filled with joy. And everywhere they went, in the Temple and in the synagogues, they gave praise to God.

SENT OUT ON A MISSION

To live the Mass is good. To share it with others is even better! When the priest dismisses us at the end of the Mass, he bids us to do as Jesus asked his Apostles. "Go! Make disciples of all nations!" said Christ before ascending to his Father. Let's not keep to ourselves this joy we have just received in hearing the Word of God and receiving Communion. For the word "Mass" means "mission."

THE FIRST CHRISTIAN COMMUNITIES

PROCLAIMING THE GOOD NEWS

THE APOSTLES SENT OUT ON MISSION

Before ascending to his Father, Jesus gathered his Apostles and sent them out on mission: *Go therefore and make disciples of all nations, baptizing them in the name of the Father and of the Son and of the Holy Spirit* (Matthew 28:19). This is the Good News about the New Covenant: it is offered to everyone on earth. The Apostles were to set out toward all corners of the world to spread this Good News: Jesus died and rose again to save us from sin. The Acts of the Apostles, also written by Saint Luke, tells their story.

THE GIFT OF THE SPIRIT

The Apostles felt afraid after the Ascension. But Jesus sent his Holy Spirit, the Spirit of strength, so that they could overcome their fears and set out on their mission. On the day of Pentecost, while they were in the Upper Room behind locked doors, the Spirit descended upon them. The Apostles were filled with a new strength that urged them forward. It supported their faith and gave them the courage and the words to go out evangelizing. From then on, no obstacle could stop them, not even death.

THE FIRST COMMUNITIES...

The first Christians—those who identified themselves with Christ—were nearly all converted Jews. Jesus' Apostles and many disciples began by forming a community in Jerusalem. They then addressed themselves to Jews living abroad, in Greece, Syria, Egypt, and Rome, sending them Apostles. More and more communities were born. Then Jesus' message reached the pagans, who also converted: first the pagans of Judea, then those in neighboring lands. Saint Paul tirelessly wrote to them.

...AND THE FIRST MARTYRS

The number of conversions had many people wringing their hands in frustration. The Jewish leaders who rejected Jesus were furious that his death hadn't been enough to stop these new believers. For their part, the Romans feared public disorder. Unbelieving Jews and Romans persecuted Christians, and sometimes even put them to death. Young Stephen was the first to lose his life in the name of Jesus: he was the first martyr.

THROUGHOUT THE WHOLE ROMAN EMPIRE

In the time of the first Christians, not everyone was in agreement. Most of them were converted Jews who continued to observe the Law. But what to do about converted pagans? Should they too observe Jewish Law? The Apostle Paul was clear: no! Faith in Jesus was more important than the fine points of the Law. From then on, the Christian faith quickly spread even further throughout the pagan world, and in the Roman Empire in particular. Communities sprang up in many cities all around the Mediterranean Sea.

VICTIMS FOR THEIR FAITH

This new religion was not at all to the liking of the Romans. It worried them more and more. They feared it might set off more uprisings and threaten the peace of the empire. To stamp out this menace, they began tracking down and persecuting Christians. Anyone who dared to proclaim Jesus' message was arrested and killed. One by one, Jesus' Apostles died in martyrdom, all except John.

THE EARLY CHURCH

Persecutions were not enough to stop the people's great drive toward the Christian faith. Quite the opposite! The more Christians were persecuted, the more it seemed to strengthen the faith of their brethren. Little by little, small groups organized into "churches," a word that in Greek means "assemblies of those called." To unite and guide the people, the Apostles appointed successors to head these churches. They were called bishops. To the successor of Peter, to whom Jesus had entrusted the Church, they gave the name "pope."

AWAITING CHRIST'S RETURN

Jesus promised that he would be with mankind until the end of time. He also promised that he would return in glory. Ever since his Ascension into heaven, to this very day Christians await this return in hope, striving to remain prepared like the faithful servant who awaits the return of his master. *Watch therefore, for you know neither the day nor the hour* (Matthew 25:13).

Sophie de Mullenheim is a prolific children's book author and a mother. She has worked as a journalist for children's presses, and, over the past fifteen years, she has authored various books, notably novels.

Fabienne Py-Renaudie holds a doctorate in religious history. While studying children's literature, she has most notably undertaken research into Bibles and saints from the 19th and 20th centuries.

Fr. François Campagnac is a priest passionate about the Bible who enjoys reading and telling Bible stories. He is in charge of youth and young adult ministry for his diocese.

Fr. Christophe Raimbault, a graduate of the French Biblical and Archeological School of Jerusalem, is a parish priest and youth pastor. He is a commentator on the Bible, heads his diocesan house of vocations, and is a teaching assistant at the Catholic Institute of Paris, France.

Adeline Avril is an illustrator. A graduate of the Emile Cohl School in Lyon, she began as a fresco painter, later turning to the illustration of children's books. She was awarded the prize for children's illustration at the 2015 Bulle d'or Festival in France.

Printed in January 2019 by Tien Wah Press, Malaysia.
Job number MGN 19001.
Printed in compliance with
the Consumer Protection Safety Act, 2008.